Cambridge Experience Readers

Level 2

Series editor: Nicholas Tims

Grandad's Magic Gadgets

Helen Everett-Camplin

CAMBRIDGE
UNIVERSITY PRESS

Shaftesbury Road, Cambridge CB2 8EA, United Kingdom

One Liberty Plaza, 20th Floor, New York, NY 10006, USA

477 Williamstown Road, Port Melbourne, VIC 3207, Australia

314–321, 3rd Floor, Plot 3, Splendor Forum, Jasola District Centre,
New Delhi – 110025, India

103 Penang Road, #05-06/07, Visioncrest Commercial, Singapore 238467

José Abascal, 56–1º, 28003 Madrid, Spain

Cambridge University Press & Assessment is a department of the
University of Cambridge.

We share the University's mission to contribute to society through the pursuit of
education, learning and research at the highest international levels of excellence.

www.cambridge.org
Information on this title: www.cambridge.org/9788483235225

© Cambridge University Press & Assessment 2010

First published 2009

41 40 39 38 37 36 35 34 33 32 31 30 29 28 27 26 25

Printed in Spain by Pulmen

ISBN 978-84-8323-522-5 Paperback; legal deposit: S.930-2009

No character in this work is based on any person living or dead.
Any resemblance to an actual person or situation is purely accidental.

Illustrations by Mikela Prevost

Audio recording by BraveArts, S.L.

Exercises by Peter McDonnell

Contents

People in the story

Marvin: a thirteen-year-old schoolboy
Tyson: a bully at Marvin's school
Grandad: Marvin's grandad
Mum: Marvin's mum
Headmaster: the man in charge of Marvin's school
Robert: a new student at Marvin's school

BEFORE YOU READ

1 Look at the cover and the pictures in the first two chapters. Answer the questions.

   1 Who are the main characters in the story?

   2 Can you see three things that Grandad has made?

Chapter 1

Escape from bed

'It's happening again, Mum,' Marvin shouted.

There was no reply.

Marvin was going to be late for school and it was all because of Grandad. Grandad and his mad[1] gadgets.[2]

Marvin looked up at the clock on his bedroom wall. The clock was one of Grandad's mad gadgets. It didn't say 'Quarter Past Eight' which was the real time. It said 'Quarter Past Shower Time' because Marvin usually had his shower at eight o'clock. Marvin shouted again.

'Mum. Can you help me? I can't get out of bed.'

Still no reply from downstairs. Marvin slowly counted to ten and then screamed as loudly as he could, 'HELLO. CAN ANYBODY HEAR ME?'

Nobody could. Grandad was making too much noise in the garage. He always made a lot of noise when he was making his gadgets.

Marvin's bed was another of Grandad's mad gadgets. Every morning at eight o'clock, the bed woke up and tidied the blankets so Marvin didn't have to. The problem was that today Marvin woke up at quarter *past* eight, so the bed tried to tidy him up[3] too.

The blanket on the bed didn't want to let him go, so he couldn't move his arms and legs. He was like a banana, waiting for someone to come and eat him or like toothpaste in a tube, waiting for someone to push him out.

'Am I more like a banana or toothpaste?' he thought.

5

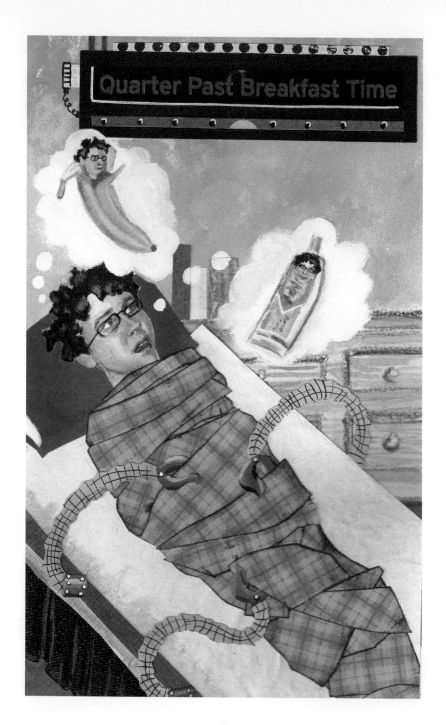

Marvin could not decide which, but he knew that this was a very important question.

He closed his eyes. 'Maybe I'm more like a banana in a toothpaste tube or perhaps toothpaste in a banana skin. Mmm, banana toothpaste—'

'Marvin, get up. It's time for school.'

Mum's loud voice ended Marvin's daydreams about fruit toothpaste. She was calling him from the kitchen.

'But Mum …' he shouted.

She didn't hear him. The clock now said 'Quarter Past Breakfast Time' and Marvin decided to try again to get out of bed.

'One, two, three, pull,' said Marvin, as he tried to pull his arms out from under the blanket. But the blanket did not let him go.

'One, two, three, push,' said Marvin, as he tried to push the blanket away with his feet. But the blanket still did not let him go.

He couldn't do it. The bed was stronger than he was.

'I think I'll go back to sleep,' thought Marvin. 'It's better than going to school.'

Marvin didn't really like school at the moment. Tyson was at school and he was a big bully[4]. And Tyson liked to bully Marvin more than anyone else at school. Yes, it was better if he stayed in bed. He closed his eyes.

'Marvin, you're going to be late for school.'

Mum's voice was loud and angry. Marvin heard her coming upstairs. Then his bedroom door opened and she was standing in front of him.

'Get up now, Marvin!'

'I can't,' cried Marvin. 'The bed woke up at eight o'clock

and tidied the blankets. I was still sleeping, so it tidied me too! Now I can't get out.'

'Oh Marvin. Not again.'

Mum quickly started to pull at the blankets. She could not move them.

'Let my son go,' she shouted at the blankets. 'You can stay in bed all day but he can't. He's got to go to school.'

'Talking to them won't help, Mum,' said Marvin quietly. 'You have to turn them off at the wall.'

Mum pushed a button next to Marvin's bed. As soon as she did this, the blankets let Marvin go.

'Thanks, Mum,' said Marvin. 'I thought I was never going to escape.'

'Why didn't you shout for help?'

'I did. Nobody heard me.'

'Sorry, love,' said Mum. 'I can't hear anything downstairs. Your grandad is making things in the garage again and the noise is terrible.'

'It's always noisy now that Grandad is living with us,' replied Marvin, just as the clock changed to 'Walk To School Time'.

Marvin looked out of his bedroom window. He could see Grandad working in his garage. He was pulling the front off Mum's old TV! Marvin watched with his mouth open as Grandad started to hit the TV with his big hammer. Pieces of glass and old TV were flying all around the garage.

'He's trying to help us, Marvin. You know that,' said Mum, as Marvin moved quickly away from the window. 'It's just that … well … it's just that the gadgets aren't always very good, are they? Like your bed—'

'Which stops me from getting up,' Marvin finished her sentence.

'Or the clock—' Mum continued.

'Which can't tell the time,' Marvin said.

'Or the singing shower—'

'Which has a terrible voice.'

'Or the toilet—'

'Which talks to you all the time.'

Soon Marvin and his mum were laughing.

'Life is more fun now that Grandad is living here,' said Marvin.

'That's true,' said his mum. 'Oh, and Marvin …'

'Yes, Mum.'

'Stop reading in bed. That's why you woke up late this morning.'

'How did you know?' asked Marvin.

'Mums know everything,' his mum replied. 'And you were still wearing your glasses when you woke up.' She smiled at him. 'Now, get ready for school or you really will be late.'

'Can I wear my new trainers[5]?' Marvin asked.

'If you promise[6] to look after them.'

'Thanks, Mum,' smiled Marvin, who felt that the day was better already.

But as he left his bedroom that morning, wearing his new trainers, he didn't see that the clock was now saying 'DANGER TIME!'

Chapter 2

Tyson the terrible

When Marvin arrived in the kitchen, Grandad was sitting at the table, drinking tea and smiling a big smile. His hair was grey and his face had lots of lines on it, but he looked very young when he smiled. And he was almost always smiling.

Today he was wearing a big hat with five different pairs of glasses all around it. Grandad needed different glasses for different things. He needed them for reading, for looking at people, for using the Internet, for sitting in the sun and, of course, for making things. When he needed to change his glasses, he just turned his hat to the left or the right. So he never lost his glasses like other grandads sometimes did.

'Good morning, Favourite Grandson!' Grandad said as Marvin quickly ate his breakfast. 'You're in a hurry this morning!'

'I woke up late,' said Marvin. 'The bed didn't let me get up.'

But Grandad didn't hear him. He was already walking to the garage and thinking about making his next mad gadget. 'Have a great day at school,' he shouted as he left.

'Bye, Grandad,' smiled Marvin. 'Have a great day in the garage.'

Marvin left home feeling happy. He was listening to his favourite music on his MP3 player and he was wearing his new trainers.

'And I've got a swimming class later. I love swimming. Today is going to be a good day,' he thought.

He danced along the street to the music.

'Hey, Marilyn!'

Tyson's voice cut through Marvin's happiness like a knife. Marvin knew it was Tyson because his voice was very loud and because he always called Marvin by a girl's name. Tyson thought this was funny.

'What's wrong with you, Marilyn?'

Marvin stopped his little dance and started to walk quickly towards school.

Tyson followed him.

'Hey, Marilyn. I'm talking to you' Tyson said behind him.

Tyson pushed his finger into Marvin's back. Marvin turned to look at him. Tyson was smiling but it wasn't a nice smile.

'Didn't you hear me, Marilyn?'

'I thought you were talking to somebody else. My name's *Marvin*,' he replied. 'And anyway, I was listening to my music.'

Tyson took Marvin's MP3 player from him and listened. 'What's that? Classical music?' he laughed.

Marvin looked down at his feet and tried to think of something to say. Tyson looked down at the same time.

'Ah,' he said. 'Were you dancing in your little new trainers?'

Marvin found his voice. 'I wasn't dancing. I was doing my fighting practice.'

'Little Marilyn can fight?' Tyson laughed in Marvin's face. 'Don't talk to me about fighting. See this scar?'

He showed Marvin his arm. It had a big long line on it with lots of smaller lines across it.

'Yes,' said Marvin. He knew what Tyson was going to say next.

'I got this when I stopped five robbers from robbing a bank. I'm not afraid of anyone or anything.'

'You said there were three robbers last time,' Marvin said. He quickly took his MP3 player back from Tyson and started to run away.

But Tyson was already leaving. Some other students were coming towards them and he knew that they always looked after Marvin.

'Be careful today, fighting boy,' he shouted as he left. 'I'll be right behind you.'

Marvin was so angry he had stomach ache. Tyson always made him feel bad. And every time that Tyson was horrible to Marvin, Marvin's stomach hurt.

*   *   *

Lessons in the morning were boring, but after lunch Marvin had swimming class. Marvin got ready in the changing rooms at school and put his bag, clothes and new trainers in his school locker. As he locked his locker, Tyson came into the changing rooms. He was right behind Marvin. Marvin quickly took his towel and ran out of the room. He didn't want any more trouble[7] from Tyson.

Tyson looked around him. There was no one in the changing rooms – no one to bully. He was just leaving when he saw some keys in one of the lockers – Marvin's locker.

'Excellent,' thought Tyson as he opened the door.

Inside were Marvin's bag, clothes and … his new

trainers! Tyson quickly took the trainers out and closed the door again. Then he put Marvin's key in his pocket.

A few minutes later he was standing outside the swimming pool and waving at Marvin through the window. Marvin wasn't wearing his glasses and his eyes were full of water, so he couldn't see what was in Tyson's hand at first. He climbed out of the swimming pool, dried his eyes and put his glasses on. Then he saw everything.

'No!' shouted Marvin. 'Not my new trainers.'

He put his towel around him and ran outside as quickly as he could. He knew he was quicker than Tyson but, of course, Tyson was wearing shoes and Marvin wasn't.

Marvin was wet and cold and his feet were hurting, but soon he could see Tyson, who was running towards the school café.

'Oh no!' thought Marvin. 'I think he's going to throw[8] my trainers in the dustbin.[9]'

He was right. When he arrived at the café, he saw Tyson throwing his trainers into the big dustbin outside the school kitchen. His lovely new trainers were now under vegetables, tomatoes, old bits of meat and fish. Marvin quickly pulled them out but they were not clean now. No. Now they had bits of food on them and were very, very dirty.

Tyson thought this was very funny.

'Hey, Marilyn!,' he shouted. 'You've got very dirty feet. Your trainers were clean this morning!'

Marvin thought he was going to cry.

Tyson put his hand over his nose and came across to Marvin.

'Your feet are very smelly[10] too. Your trainers smell like old fish!'

He ran away, still laughing.

Marvin was very angry now, so his stomach was hurting again. He wanted to run after Tyson and fight him. But he knew that was stupid. He was smaller than Tyson and he was also wet and wearing only a towel. He started to walk slowly back to the changing rooms in his dirty trainers.

As he turned the corner, he saw Tyson again. The bully was standing in the playground. He wasn't moving. There was a big angry dog outside the school gates. It was jumping up and down and making a lot of noise. Marvin could see that Tyson's face was very white. He was shaking[11] all over and holding his stomach. As Marvin got closer, Tyson's face changed from white to green and then he was sick all over his shoes.

'So, Tyson *is* afraid of something,' thought Marvin as he walked away. 'And I'm not the only person who has to clean his shoes tonight.'

LOOKING BACK

1 Check your answers to *Before you read* on page 4.

ACTIVITIES

2 Match the two parts of the sentences.

1 Marvin doesn't like school because [c]
2 Marvin and Mum are happier now because ☐
3 Marvin is happy today because ☐
4 Marvin's new trainers are smelly because ☐

a Grandad is living with them.
b Tyson has thrown them in the dustbin.
c Tyson is unfriendly to him.
d he's got a swimming class.

3 Complete the sentences with the names in the box.

| Marvin (x4)   Tyson   Grandad (x2)   Mum |

1 _Marvin_ doesn't have to make his bed.
2 .... helps Marvin escape from his bed.
3 .... has got new trainers.
4 .... makes a lot of noise in the garage.
5 .... makes mad gadgets.
6 .... has a very loud voice.
7 .... listens to classical music on his MP3 player.
8 .... can run faster than Tyson.

20

4 Are the sentences true (*T*) or false (*F*)?

1 Marvin has a shower at seven o'clock. $\boxed{F}$
2 Grandad made Marvin's bed. ☐
3 Marvin wears his new trainers to go to school. ☐
4 Grandad doesn't need to wear glasses. ☐
5 Tyson calls Marvin 'Marlon'. ☐
6 Tyson takes Marvin's new hat. ☐
7 Tyson is bigger than Marvin. ☐
8 Marvin feels sick when he sees an angry dog. ☐

5 Answer the questions.

1 Why doesn't Mum hear Marvin calling her?

2 What does Marvin's shower do?

3 What does Tyson tell Marvin about his arm?

4 What happens to Marvin when Tyson is unkind to him?

LOOKING FORWARD

6 Tick (✓) what you think happens in the next two chapters.

1 Grandad puts a gadget on Marvin's trainers. ☐
2 Grandad cleans Marvin's trainers. ☐
3 Grandad buys Marvin new trainers. ☐

Chapter 3

The trainers talk too much

Marvin woke up at 'Quarter To Shower' time. The bed was still asleep, so he got up quickly.

He heard his mum and his grandad talking together, but he could hear another voice too. Who was visiting this early in the morning?

He quickly ran into the bathroom to get ready.

'Good morning, Marvin,' said the toilet. 'Nice to see you again.'

'Nice to see you too,' said Marvin. He always felt very stupid talking to a toilet.

'Standing or sitting, sir?'

'Standing, please,' said Marvin and the toilet seat went up.

'Thank you,' said Marvin when he finished. Then he turned the shower on.

'La–la–la–la–la, la–la–la–la–la.' The shower started singing in a loud and very bad voice.

Marvin stood under the shower. He turned the water from 'cold' to 'hot'.

'Oh–oh–oh–oh,' sang the shower in a higher, but still very bad, voice.

Marvin put his fingers in his ears, but he could still hear the terrible noise, so he had his shower very quickly. Then he put his clothes on and hurried to see who was in the kitchen. But when he got there, he could see only Mum and Grandad. Mum was washing up. Grandad was sitting at the kitchen table, drinking tea and wearing his usual hat. Today Grandad was also wearing his 'gadget jacket'. It was big and red and had pockets all over it. The pockets were full of tools for making things. Marvin didn't know the names of most of them. Grandad usually wore his gadget jacket when he was making something new.

'Good morning, Favourite Grandson!' Grandad smiled his big smile.

Marvin smiled back. 'Who were you talking to just now, Grandad?'

'I was talking to your new trainers,' said Grandad and he opened a box on the kitchen table.

Marvin looked into the box. They were his *old* trainers, but they looked different. They each had a big red button on the end. Marvin took one of the trainers from the box.

'Don't push that button!' shouted Grandad.

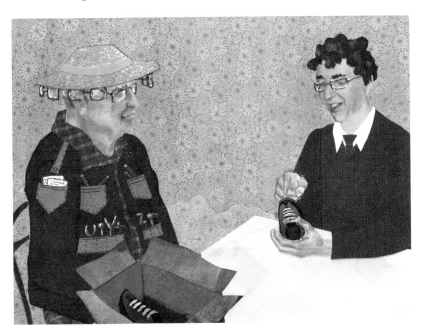

Too late. The trainer shouted 'Get off!' very loudly and Marvin dropped[12] it on the floor.

Grandad picked the trainer up[13] and pushed the button again. The trainer stopped shouting.

'Push that button when you take your trainers off,' Grandad said. 'Then if someone else takes them, they will shout for help. See?'

Grandad pushed the red button on the second trainer. It shouted 'Stop! Help!'

Grandad smiled and gave the trainers back to Marvin.

'They won't talk while I'm wearing them, will they?' Marvin asked.

'Only if you push the buttons,' Grandad replied.

'These are great, Grandad. Thank you,' said Marvin. He kissed his grandad and his mum and left for school.

Before his swimming class Marvin put the trainers with his other clothes in the locker, but he couldn't find his locker key. 'Oh well,' he thought. 'They'll be safe now.' He pushed the red buttons, shut the locker door and went for his swim.

A few minutes later Tyson walked into the changing room. He still had Marvin's locker key in his pocket but he saw that the door was already open.

'This is too easy,' he smiled to himself, as he took the shoes from the locker. But he soon stopped smiling.

'Get off!' shouted one of the trainers.

'Help!' shouted the other trainer.

Tyson was so surprised that he dropped the trainers. He also dropped his water bottle and water went all over the trainers. He pushed them back into the locker and locked it with Marvin's key.

The trainers were very wet. They stopped shouting for a few seconds. Then something went very wrong.

'It's dark in here,' said one trainer, 'I'm afraid.'

'Me too,' said the other trainer.

'Let me out!' shouted the first trainer.

'Let me out too!' shouted the other trainer.

At that moment the headmaster walked past.

'Hello!' shouted the trainers, together this time.

'Hello,' replied the headmaster. 'Who's there?'

'We want to get out!' shouted the trainers.

'We? We? How many of you are in there?' asked the headmaster as he tried to open the locker door.

'Help!' shouted the trainers again.

Now lots of students were standing around and watching.

'Move away!' said the headmaster. 'There are two students in the locker. I'm going to break the door and get them out!'

At that moment Marvin came into the changing room wearing only his towel.

'What's happening?' he asked another boy.

'There are students in that locker,' the boy replied.

Marvin pushed through the students. At that moment,

the headmaster pulled the door off the locker.

'That's *my* locker!' shouted Marvin.

'And are these your trainers, Marvin?'

The headmaster had a very wet pair of trainers in his hand. The trainers were still talking, but much more quietly now.

'That's better,' said one trainer.

'Yes, that's much better. Thank you!' said the other trainer.

'Yes, they're mine,' Marvin said quietly. 'But I don't know how they got wet.'

'Your trainers are talking,' said the headmaster.

'Yes. Sorry.'

'Sorry? Sorry? That's not good enough. I think you need to write an essay.'

'An essay?' said Marvin. He knew things were bad. The headmaster only asked students to write an essay when they were in big trouble.

'Yes, I want you to write five hundred words about "Why shoes are for walking, not for talking". And I want you to put it on my desk tomorrow morning.'

The other students were leaving. There was nothing more to see. Marvin pushed the red buttons on his wet trainers, but they didn't stop talking.

'I'll have to walk home in them. I'm sure they'll stop when they are dry,' Marvin thought.

But the shoes didn't stop talking. Oh, no. All the way from the school to his house, the shoes talked and talked and talked.

'Another one of Grandad's mad gadgets,' Marvin said to himself, unhappily.

Chapter 4

Marvin the rock star

When Marvin got home that night, he went to the garage. He could see Grandad through the open door. He was moving around the garage in a very strange way. Was he dancing?

'Grandad,' he shouted.

Grandad waved at Marvin. 'I'm sorry. I can't hear you. I'll take these glasses off.'

Marvin didn't understand how taking your glasses off could help anyone to hear, but Grandad wasn't just anyone.

'Now then, Favourite Grandson. What can I do for you?'

'You can stop my trainers talking all the time,' said Marvin and he told Grandad about his day at school. 'And now I've got to write five hundred words about why shoes are for walking, not for talking.'

'I'm sorry, Marvin,' said Grandad sadly. 'I was only trying to help.'

'I know and I love your gadgets,' Marvin said quickly. But he was just being kind. He didn't like it when Grandad was sad.

'Good!' shouted Grandad with a smile. 'Because these are for you.'

He gave Marvin the glasses.

'But these are just my *old* glasses,' said Marvin. 'I've got new ones now.'

'Yes, but I changed a few things,' said Grandad excitedly. 'Put them on.'

Marvin thought Grandad was mad, but he put the old glasses on.

'Now, push the button on the nose.'

Marvin pushed a small button on the nose of his glasses and in a second his head was full of music. Wonderful classical music. He soon forgot about Tyson. He forgot about the trainers. He forgot about his essay. The music was not just inside his ears, but inside his head, his hands and his feet. He felt wonderful.

Then Grandad took the glasses off Marvin's head and everything went back to normal again.

'You push the nose of the glasses to turn it on and off, the left side to make it go louder and the right side to change the music – from classical to rock.'

'I'll never change the music,' said Marvin.

'OK. But remember, "Nose – on, nose – off, left – loud, right – rock". Yes?'

'Nose – on, nose – off, left – loud, right – rock,' Marvin repeated. 'I understand. Thank you, Grandad.'

Grandad smiled his big smile. 'You're welcome,[14] Favourite Grandson.'

∗   ∗   ∗

At lunchtime the next day Marvin was sitting outside, eating his sandwiches and reading a book. His essay was on the headmaster's desk and he was happy with life. He pushed the nose of his glasses and beautiful music came into his ears and right through his body. He closed his eyes and his head moved slowly from side to side. He felt great. He was enjoying the music so much that he didn't see Tyson running past with a football.

BANG! – the football hit Marvin on the left side of his head. Left was for loud, so the music got louder. Marvin jumped up and saw Tyson a few metres away. He was laughing.

'I shouted "Catch". Can't you hear me?' he said.

But Marvin couldn't hear him because the music was very loud now.

He wanted to throw the football back, but his body couldn't do it. The music was loud and strong and it was inside his body. His arms and legs were moving to the music. His feet were jumping up and down and his head was moving from side to side.

'Nose – on, nose – off,' thought Marvin trying to push the button on his nose. But his hands waved around his head.

'Nose – on, nose – off,' Marvin tried again but his hand hit the right side of his glasses.

'Oh no! Right is for rock music!' thought Marvin.

Two seconds later, his body was still moving to the music but much, much faster. His arms and legs danced when the guitar made a noise. His head moved when the keyboard played. His body jumped and danced and turned around to the music. He was still trying very hard to take his glasses off so he could stop dancing. But his hands were enjoying the music and they were not interested in helping him.

The other students watched him with their mouths open.

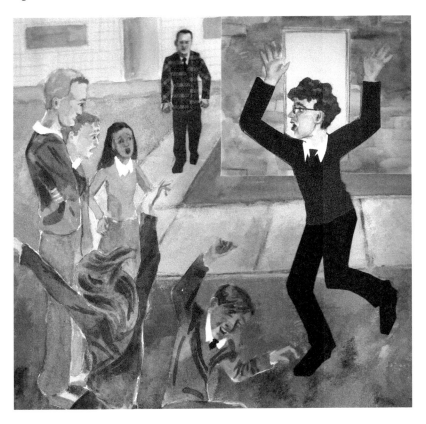

'Look at Marvin,' they were saying. 'He's a really good dancer. He looks like a rock star.'

Then they all decided to do the same. Soon the playground was full of children jumping and waving their arms and dancing.

Then the headmaster arrived. Marvin's classmates stopped dancing. Marvin, of course, didn't. He couldn't.

The headmaster shouted at him. Marvin waved his arms.

The headmaster stood in front of him. Marvin jumped up and down.

The headmaster shook his finger at him. Marvin shook his head from side to side.

Everyone watched as Marvin shook his head. Up and down. Left and right. Marvin was shaking his head so much that … ah, at last … his glasses fell off.

No more music. No more keyboards. No more guitars. No more noise. Just the sound of the headmaster saying, 'Marvin. I want you to write another essay. One thousand words on "Why I am a student not a rock star".' Put it on my desk before your maths test on Friday.

One thousand words! And all because of Grandad's mad gadgets. Marvin was very angry.

He became even angrier as he sat in his bedroom later that night writing his essay. His hands were hurting and he was tired, so he was making lots of mistakes.

He looked at the clock. 'Two Hours Past Bed Time', it said.

'Right. That's it. I've had enough,' he said to himself.

He went downstairs to the garage and left a note[15] for Grandad. It said:

Write an essay of one thousand words on 'Why I must stop making stupid gadgets for Marvin.'

Then he went to bed, still feeling very angry.

LOOKING BACK

1 Check your answer to *Looking forward* on page 21.

ACTIVITIES

2 Are the sentences true (*T*) or false (*F*)?

1 The toilet talks to Marvin. ☐T
2 Mum is cooking in the kitchen. ☐
3 Grandad was talking to Marvin's mum in the kitchen. ☐
4 Marvin leaves his trainers in the classroom. ☐
5 Tyson has got the key to Marvin's locker. ☐
6 The trainers get wet. ☐
7 The headmaster tells Tyson to write an essay. ☐
8 Marvin's trainers don't stop talking. ☐

3 Match the two parts of the sentences.

1 The trainers are afraid because ☐c
2 The headmaster breaks the locker door because ☐
3 Marvin hasn't done anything wrong in the changing room but ☐
4 Marvin puts his musical glasses on and ☐
5 The music from the glasses ☐
6 Marvin feels very angry ☐

a he has to write an essay.
b he forgets about his problems.
c it's dark in the locker.
d he thinks there are students in there.
e with his grandad.
f makes Marvin's body move.

4 What do the <u>underlined</u> words refer to in these lines from the text?

1 '<u>They</u>'ll be safe now.' (page 24) ...... *the trainers* ......

2 'It's dark in <u>here</u>,' said one trainer. (page 25) ....

3 'And I want you to put <u>it</u> on my desk tomorrow morning.' (page 27) ....

4 'Good' shouted Grandad with a smile, 'because <u>these</u> are for you.' (page 28) ....

5 But Marvin couldn't hear <u>him</u> because the music was very loud now. (page 30) ....

6 Then <u>he</u> went to bed, still feeling very angry. (page 33) ....

5 Answer the questions.

1 When does Grandad wear his gadget jacket?

....

2 Who opens the locker door?

....

3 What can Marvin do with his new glasses?

....

4 What does Marvin leave for Grandad?

....

LOOKING FORWARD

6 What do you think? Answer the questions.

1 What will Grandad do when he reads Marvin's note?

....

2 Grandad invents Smelly Vision. What is it?

....

Chapter 5

What's cooking?

Marvin woke up the next morning. He was still feeling angry, but he was feeling a little bit sad too. And he wasn't the only one. Grandad's gadgets seemed to be angry and sad too.

Marvin looked up at his clock to see what time it was. The clock said, 'Say Sorry Time'. Marvin turned his head away. He didn't like feeling this way, but he wasn't going to say sorry because he wasn't sorry. He hated Grandad's gadgets. They got him into trouble.

Marvin's angry feet walked into the bathroom. He stood in front of the toilet. But the toilet didn't say 'Sitting or standing?' this morning. It said, 'Say Sorry To Grandad.'

'I will not say sorry to Grandad,' Marvin thought. He stood under the shower and turned it on.

But the shower didn't sing loudly this morning. It sang a very slow, sad song. 'S–a–y S–o–r–r–y,' it sang. 'S–o–r–r–y.'

It seemed that all Grandad's gadgets were unhappy with Marvin – even his bed was still untidy – and deep inside Marvin knew why. He also knew that they were right. He decided he was going to say sorry to Grandad before he went to school.

He got dressed[16] and went downstairs. Mum was in the kitchen.

'Where's Grandad?' asked Marvin.

'He's in the garage. I think he's been there all night.'

'Oh. Didn't he go to bed?'

'No, love.'

'I need to talk to him,' Marvin said in a small voice.

'I think he needs to be by himself today,' said Mum. 'He looks very unhappy.'

So Marvin walked to school with his head full of sad thoughts. His body felt heavier than usual and his legs walked more slowly.

'Hey, Marilyn!' shouted Tyson. 'Not dancing today?'

Marvin didn't answer Tyson because he didn't hear him. He was thinking about Grandad.

'Hey!' shouted Tyson. He stood in front of Marvin.

Marvin looked up at the big bully and, to his surprise, he wasn't afraid of him today.

'Get out of my way, Tyson,' he said.

Tyson's face changed colour. For a few short seconds *he* looked afraid. Then he laughed that loud bully's laugh and said, 'I'm not afraid of you, Marilyn. You see this?'

He showed Marvin his arm again.

'I got this when I was fighting seven robbers, you know—'

But Marvin just walked away from Tyson. He was sick of listening to his stupid stories. Marvin sat quietly in class for the rest of the day and waited for school to finish. He just wanted to go home, say sorry to Grandad and get the sad thoughts out of his head.

*   *   *

When Marvin got home, the garage door was still closed. So he sat in his bedroom and tried to write his essay. Because he was feeling bad about Grandad, he was making even more mistakes than usual. It was taking a long time and his hands were hurting as much as his heart.

'Marvin. Your TV programme is starting,' his mum shouted up the stairs.

Marvin ran into the living room. His grandad was watching TV.

'Hello, Favourite Grandson,' said Grandad.

'I'm so sorry, Grandad,' Marvin replied and he put his arms around him.

Grandad smiled at Marvin and everything in life seemed OK again. Marvin's feet weren't angry, his body wasn't heavy and his head was full of happy thoughts again.

Marvin's favourite cooking programme was starting.

'Today I'm making chocolate cake,' said the chef on the TV. Marvin watched carefully as the chef started to make the cake. Suddenly, Marvin thought he *could smell* chocolate. He sniffed[17] the air. Yes, he *could* smell chocolate!

He ran into the kitchen to see if his mum was making a cake, but she was reading a magazine. He ran back into the living room. The smell of chocolate was getting stronger and Grandad's smile was getting bigger.

'What's happening?' Marvin asked his grandad.

'Welcome to Smelly Vision,' said Grandad. 'I finished working on it last night. Now you can watch TV and smell it at the same time.'

'What!' said Marvin. 'How can you smell a TV?'

Grandad smiled. 'You smell what you see. There is a special button so you can make the smell stronger or weaker, just like the sound. The chef is making chocolate cake, so you can smell chocolate now, but if you watch something else the smells change.'

Grandad changed the channel on the TV. It was a programme about gardens. At that moment, the room filled

with the smell of grass and flowers.

'And if you don't like the smell, you can just turn it off,' he said. And he pushed another button. The smell of grass slowly went away.

'This is fantastic,' said Marvin. 'I'm sorry I said your gadgets were stupid. I *love* them.'

'Good,' said Grandad, 'because I've got another one for you.'

He gave Marvin a small white piece of plastic. 'It's a rubber,' he said. 'You can use it when you're writing your essay. It will take the mistakes away.'

'But, Grandad, I've already got a rubber,' Marvin said. He didn't understand.

'Ah, but you don't have a rubber like this one,' said Grandad. 'Watch.'

He wrote some words on a piece of paper and put the rubber on the table. 'Rub it,' he said. The rubber started moving across the paper and taking the words away. 'Stop,' said Grandad and the rubber stopped moving.

'Thank you very much, Grandad. It's just what I need.'

Marvin ran up to his bedroom feeling quite excited. Yesterday, Grandad's gadgets brought him nothing but problems, but now he thought they were wonderful. He looked at his new rubber before he put it with the pencils in his backpack.[18]

'You're going to change my life,' he said.

And he was right. But not in the way he hoped.

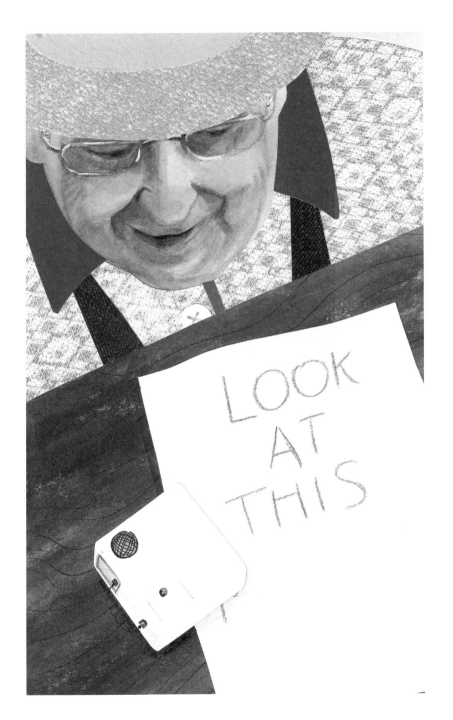

Chapter 6

Losing words and finding friends

Marvin felt very happy when he got up. He wasn't angry with Grandad any more. He had a wonderful TV that you could smell and see at the same time. And he finished his essay last night. It was much quicker with the new rubber.

Even thinking about the maths test today didn't make him feel bad. He hated maths and he hated tests. But today he wasn't going to have a problem if he made mistakes, because he could just say 'Rub it' very quietly and start again. Yes, today was going to be a lovely day.

His clock said 'Lots Of Time To Get Ready' so Marvin spent a long time in the bathroom. The shower sang its usual loud and happy song in its terrible voice and the toilet was speaking to him again.

He didn't meet Tyson on the way to school, so when the maths test started Marvin was feeling really good.

Grandad's rubber worked very well. Every time that Marvin made a mistake, he said 'Rub it' very quietly and the rubber moved across the page until the mistake went away. When he wanted it to stop rubbing out, he said 'Stop' very quietly and the rubber stopped. Marvin finished the test quickly. He felt very happy with himself when the teacher told the class to stop writing and he had no more questions to answer.

The headmaster walked into the class at that moment. He had a small, fair-haired boy with him.

'We have a new student at the school,' said the headmaster. 'It is his first day at school today and I want you all to meet him.'

Marvin liked the look of this new boy. 'Who knows? Maybe we could become friends,' he thought to himself.

The headmaster was still talking. 'He is going to sit next to …Marvin.'

'Yes!' thought Marvin.

'And his name is Robert.'

'Robert' sounded like 'Rub it', so the rubber started moving on Marvin's desk. But Marvin was still looking at the new boy. He didn't see the rubber as it quietly started its work.

'Maybe Robert can come to my house for tea and watch Smelly Vision,' Marvin thought. He smiled and looked down at his test paper.

Suddenly he felt very sick. His face went very white – almost as white as his test paper. Marvin couldn't believe it. Where were his first five test answers? He quickly shouted 'Stop' at the rubber. The rubber stopped moving.

'What did you say, Marvin?' The headmaster looked at him.

'Um ... nothing, sir,' Marvin said quietly.

The headmaster looked at him for a long time before he started to talk again. 'As I was saying, Robert has just moved to this town and—'

Again, the rubber heard 'Rub it', not 'Robert', and started its work again.

'Stop!' shouted Marvin. The rubber stopped. The headmaster stopped.

'Did you shout "Stop" at me, Marvin?' asked the headmaster angrily.

'No, Headmaster. Not at you. At my rubber.'

Everyone in the class started laughing. Everyone except the headmaster.

'You shouted "Stop" at your rubber? Mmm, your trainers talk and your glasses play music. And now you tell me you shout at your rubber? Don't be stupid, boy, or I'll give you another essay to do.'

'Sorry, sir,' said Marvin quickly. He really didn't want another essay to write. His hands were still hurting after last night. He looked down at his test paper. Now there were only a few answers on the page.

'So, I want everyone to say a big "Hello" to Robert,' the headmaster said.

All the class shouted 'Hello, Robert,' and the rest of Marvin's answers went away in two seconds. Marvin put his head on his desk. He wanted to cry.

'Marvin?' The headmaster was looking down at him. 'Move your things so that Robert can sit next to you.'

The headmaster picked up Marvin's test paper. He

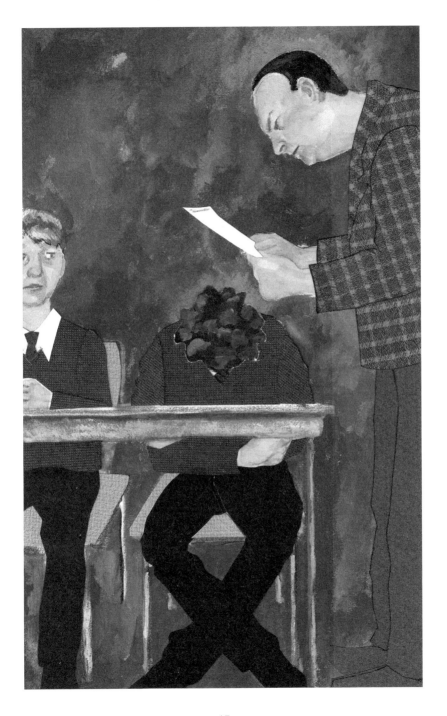

looked at the front and then he looked at the back. There were no answers anywhere.

'You haven't answered any questions!' he shouted. 'Why not?'

Marvin knew the headmaster wasn't going to believe him, so he said nothing.

'I don't know what's wrong with you, Marvin,' said the headmaster. 'You have changed in the past few weeks. Come and see me in my office later.'

'Yes, sir,' Marvin replied sadly.

Robert smiled a friendly smile. 'Bad luck,[19]' he said quietly.

Marvin smiled back.

'Can I have lunch with you?' asked Robert. 'I want to hear all about your talking trainers and your musical glasses and …' he picked up Marvin's rubber, '… why you talk to your rubber.'

So Marvin and Robert went to the school café and, at lunch, Marvin told Robert about Grandad and his gadgets. Robert thought they sounded great. Marvin also told him about what happened when the gadgets went wrong. Robert thought this was very funny.

'But Smelly Vision is wonderful,' said Marvin and he told Robert all about his TV. 'It's very good when you are watching cooking programmes,' he said.

'I love cooking,' said Robert.

Marvin couldn't believe that Robert liked the same things that he did. Could he ask Robert to come round to his house?

'It's the *Food Around the World* programme on TV tonight,' he said.

'Oh. I love that,' said Robert. He looked a little shy. 'Could I watch it at your house and smell the food while I watch the programme?'

'Of course,' said Marvin with a smile and he stood up from the table and walked back to class with Robert.

A few seconds later, Tyson moved from behind the café curtains.

'Grandad's gadgets?' Tyson said to himself. 'Smelly Vision? This sounds very interesting.'

LOOKING BACK

1 Check your answers to *Looking forward* on page 35.

ACTIVITIES

2 Complete the sentences with the names in the box.

> Robert (x2)   Mum   Grandad   Marvin (x4)

1 _Marvin_ is sad on his way to school.
2 _____ says sorry to Grandad.
3 _____ is reading a magazine.
4 _____ has invented a special TV.
5 _____ uses a magic rubber for his test.
6 _____ is a new student at the school.
7 _____ wants to cry.
8 _____ says that he loves cooking.

3 Put the sentences in order.
1 Grandad shows Marvin Smelly Vision. ☐
2 Marvin tries to write his essay in his bedroom. ☐
3 Marvin decides to say sorry to Grandad. ☐1☐
4 The headmaster is angry with Marvin. ☐
5 The headmaster brings a new boy into the class. ☐
6 Marvin takes his maths test. ☐
7 Tyson hears about Smelly Vision. ☐
8 Marvin and Robert have lunch together. ☐

4 Underline the correct words in each sentence.

1 Grandad is in the garage because he _feels unhappy_ / _is making new trainers_ / _is listening to music_.

2 Marvin goes to the living room to _do his homework_ / _watch TV_ / _read a book_.

3 Grandad gives _Tyson_ / _Robert_ / _Marvin_ a rubber.

4 Marvin has got a _swimming class_ / _party_ / _maths test_ the next day.

5 Marvin tells _Robert_ / _Tyson_ / _the headmaster_ about Grandad's gadgets.

6 Marvin and Robert are going to _listen to music_ / _play football_ / _watch TV together_.

5 Answer the questions.

1 What does Marvin smell on the TV?

2 What's special about Marvin's new rubber?

3 Where do Marvin and Robert go for lunch?

4 Where is Tyson when Marvin and Robert are having lunch?

LOOKING FORWARD

6 Tick (✓) what you think happens in the next two chapters.

1 Tyson breaks some of Grandad's gadgets. ☐

2 Tyson and Marvin become friends. ☐

Chapter 7

Strange sounds and smells

It was the night of the *Food Around the World* programme, and everyone in Marvin's house was very excited.

Grandad was wearing both his gadget jacket and his hat tonight. The jacket pockets were full of tools. The hat was moving around more quickly than usual as he needed different glasses for all the things he was doing.

Mum was making sandwiches, cakes and drinks in the kitchen. She was very happy that Marvin had a new friend, so she wanted to be sure that Marvin and Robert enjoyed themselves.

Marvin and Robert were sitting in the living room watching Grandad. Robert thought Marvin's grandad seemed much more fun than most grandads he knew. When Mum walked in with the food, Grandad looked up and smiled.

'OK, boys. We're ready.'

He pushed the usual button to turn the TV on and then pushed a big red button that said 'Smell'.

'Enjoy yourselves,' he said and he left the room.

Marvin and Robert smiled at each other. Then they both turned to look at the TV. The first chef was cooking Sunday lunch and the smell of chicken filled the room. Marvin and Robert sniffed the air. 'Mmm, chicken,' they said and they both took a sandwich.

The second chef was cooking fruit pie and the smell of apples filled the room. 'Mmm, apple pie,' said Marvin and

Robert and they both took a piece of cake.

The third chef was cooking pizza and they couldn't wait to see and smell that. They were very excited.

Then they heard the doorbell. Mum went to answer it. Tyson was standing there, smiling his nicest smile.

'Come in,' said Mum. She thought he was another of Marvin's new friends.

When Tyson walked into the living room, Marvin couldn't believe it. He started to speak, but his mum was already talking.

'Make yourself at home, Tyson,' she said. 'There are sandwiches, cakes and drinks on the table.'

She left, feeling happy. But Marvin and Robert did not feel happy. Tyson put about thirty crisps in his mouth.

'Move, Marilyn,' he said and pushed his big body between Marvin and Robert.

'So, this is Smelly Vision, eh?' he said as he took the remote control from Marvin's hand.

'How do you know about Smelly Vision?' asked Marvin.

'I heard you in the school café at lunchtime,' replied Tyson. 'When you said you had Smelly Vision, I decided to come and smell it for myself. But I don't want to watch cooking.'

He pushed a button on the remote control and changed the programme.

'Ah, that's better. Football.'

Tyson put the remote control in his pocket and started to watch the football game. The room became full of the smell of grass and hot dogs and hamburgers. Marvin's stomach was hurting again. He was very angry.

'Stop it, Tyson,' he shouted. 'You're in my house now, not at school. Give me the remote control.'

'Fight me for it,' smiled Tyson. 'But remember how I got this …'

Tyson showed Robert his big scar.

'I got this fighting—' he started.

'Twenty robbers. We know,' finished Marvin, who decided at that moment that he was not afraid of Tyson any more. He jumped onto Tyson and pulled the remote control from him. Tyson couldn't believe it.

He opened his mouth to shout at Marvin but suddenly stopped. When Marvin took the remote control, he changed the programme. It wasn't football any more. It was a programme about dogs. There were dogs all over the TV screen. Big dogs and small dogs and noisy dogs with large teeth.

Tyson was very quiet.

The room was full of the smell of dogs. The smell was in Tyson's nose and in his head. He wanted to run but he couldn't. He started to shake. His face turned white and then green. He knew that if his stomach started hurting, he was going to be sick.

Robert didn't know what was happening, but Marvin did. He remembered the day he saw Tyson and the dog at school. Marvin was a kind boy, so he quickly changed the TV back to the food programme. He thought he was helping.

But he wasn't. Now the room was full of the smell of food as well as the smell of dogs. Chicken and dog. Apples and dog. Pizza and dog. It was all too much for Tyson.

'I'm going to be sick!' he cried, as he ran from the room.

'The bathroom. Quick!' shouted Marvin.

Tyson ran to the bathroom and closed the door behind him.

'Good evening, sir,' said the toilet. 'Sitting or standing?'

Tyson was very surprised and he forgot to be sick. 'I'm really ill,' he thought to himself. 'I thought the toilet talked to me.' He put his hand on the wall to stop himself falling over and by mistake he pushed the button that turned the shower on.

'La–la–la–la,' sang the shower. 'Dum–di–dum–di–dum.'

What was that terrible noise? Tyson put his fingers in his ears. Was the shower singing? He was feeling very afraid now and he hurried out of the bathroom. He ran into Grandad.

'Are you OK?' asked Grandad. He tried to find the right glasses to see Tyson better. Tyson's eyes got bigger and bigger as Grandad's big hat turned round and round.

This was too much for Tyson.

'I don't understand what's happening!' he screamed. 'I'm hearing voices and seeing things and smelling things.' He ran to the front door.

'This is a mad house!' he shouted as he ran out.

Chapter 8

Tyson tells his story

Marvin didn't sleep well that night.

Tyson wasn't nice, but Marvin felt sorry for him. Of course, he was also worried[20] about meeting Tyson at school again.

'Oh well,' he said to himself as he got up the next morning. 'It's the weekend, so I won't see him for two days.'

Feeling a little better, he walked into the kitchen. But who was that at the kitchen table? No, it couldn't be. But it was. It was … Tyson!

'T–T–T–T … ?' was all Marvin could say because he was very surprised. Where were Mum and Grandad? He began to feel afraid.

'He's angry about last night. He wants a fight. I've got to get out,' Marvin thought to himself. He started to walk back to the door.

'Morning, Marvin,' said Tyson quietly.

Marvin stopped. 'He called me "Marvin", not "Marilyn". What's wrong with him?' he said to himself.

Tyson was talking again, but Marvin wasn't listening. He was watching Tyson. He seemed smaller. Smaller and nicer. His body was the same. His face was the same. It was something inside that seemed different.

'I'm sorry about last night,' Tyson was saying.

Marvin couldn't believe it. Tyson was being kind to him! He had to sit down.

'I'm sorry about last night and I'm sorry about being

horrible to you,' Tyson continued.

Marvin and Tyson sat quietly for a long time. Marvin wasn't sure if Tyson was joking. Tyson wasn't sure if Marvin believed him. They both felt very uncomfortable. At that moment Grandad walked into the kitchen.

'Morning, Favourite Grandson,' he said in a happy voice.

'Morning, Grandad,' replied Marvin. He waited for Tyson to laugh at him because Grandad called him 'Favourite Grandson'. But Tyson just sat there.

Grandad said something quietly to Tyson and Tyson left the room.

'Where has he gone?' asked Marvin.

'To the garage,' said Grandad.

Marvin wanted to ask why, but first he said, 'He doesn't seem like Tyson at all.'

'Ah,' said Grandad. 'That's because he's *not* Tyson.'

Marvin didn't understand. 'What do you mean?'

'He's not Tyson. He's Lionel.' Grandad said.

'Lionel?'

'Yes. His mum told me.'

'When did you see his mum?'

'Last night. I was worried about Tyson because he was sick, so I followed him out of the house and walked home with him. When I met Tyson's mum, she told me everything.'

'Everything?' said Marvin.

'She told me everything about Lionel.'

'But who is Lionel?' asked Marvin again.

Tyson came back into the kitchen. 'I'm Lionel,' he said.

Tyson was now wearing a very strange blue suit. Marvin

wanted to ask him about the suit, but first he wanted to hear about 'Lionel'.

'Lionel is my real name,' said Tyson.

'But why do you call yourself Tyson?' asked Marvin.

'Because that's the name of the dog.'

'The dog?'

'The dog that bit me when I was little.'

Marvin looked at Grandad for help. Grandad shook his head and said, 'Let Tyson tell you the story.'

And Tyson did.

'When I was younger, I had a toy bear. I loved it very much.' Tyson stopped talking and looked at Marvin to see if he was laughing. He wasn't.

'Well, the boy next door was a big bully. He laughed at me for having a toy bear. One day when I wasn't looking, he gave it to his dog, Tyson. I tried to get it back and the dog bit me.'

'That's how you got your scar!' said Marvin.

Tyson's face went red. 'Yes.'

'But why do you call yourself Tyson?' asked Marvin. 'That was the dog's name!'

'I decided that I wanted to be like that dog. He wasn't afraid of anything.' Tyson's eyes were wet. 'A bully isn't afraid of anything,' he continued. 'I just wanted to feel better.'

'You bullied me,' said Marvin quietly. 'Did you feel better?'

'No,' said Tyson in a small voice. 'I'm sorry. I knew I was hurting you, but I couldn't stop myself.'

They both felt very uncomfortable again and didn't speak for a long time.

Then suddenly Marvin said,

'So that's why you're afraid of dogs!'

'Not any more,' said Grandad, smiling his big smile. 'I've made him a special suit, so now dogs will be afraid of him!'

Marvin stood next to Tyson so he could see the suit better. It was very strange. It had lots of little tubes running through it with water inside. And there was a very strong smell of soap.

'What is the thing that dogs are most afraid of?' asked Grandad.

'I don't know,' said Marvin.

'Baths!' shouted Grandad. 'I've made Lionel a suit with bath water in it. No dog will want to come near him now.'

Marvin sniffed the suit again. Yes, it really smelled of baths.

'Why don't you both walk over to Robert's house? You can see how the suit works,' said Grandad.

So Marvin and Tyson left the house. Marvin was wearing his jeans and T-shirt and Tyson was wearing his new suit.

It felt strange to be walking next to Tyson and not running away from him. But Marvin was happy. Now he had two new friends. He turned to smile at Tyson, but Tyson couldn't see him. He was looking at a big black dog.

The dog was running towards them. It had very large teeth and it was making a loud noise. Tyson felt afraid and he closed his eyes. Marvin felt afraid but he kept his eyes open. When the dog was a few metres away, it stopped running and put its nose in the air. It sniffed loudly. Then it made a noise like a little baby and quickly jumped over a wall and ran away.

Marvin laughed and turned to Tyson. 'It's OK,' he said. 'The dog has gone.'

Tyson opened his eyes. 'What happened?' he asked.

'The dog was afraid of you,' said Marvin. 'The suit worked!'

'That's fantastic!' said Tyson. 'I love this suit!'

He looked down at the tubes of soap and water in his jacket. 'It's a bit mad,' he said, 'like your toilet and your shower—'

'And my trainers and my glasses,' said Marvin.

'Yes. Mad but a little bit magic too.' Tyson said.

Marvin watched his new friend walk along in his new blue suit. Each time Tyson moved his legs, bubbles came up through the bottom of his jacket. Soon the street behind him was full of small bubbles and big dogs running away. Marvin started to laugh.

'Yes,' he agreed. 'A little bit mad and a little bit magic. Just like my life since Grandad came to stay. Grandad and his magic gadgets!'

LOOKING BACK

1 Check your answer to *Looking forward* on page 49.

ACTIVITIES

2 Put the sentences in order.

  1 Tyson arrives at Marvin's house. ☐

  2 Marvin and Robert watch Smelly Vision together. ☐*1*

  3 The toilet and shower talk to Tyson. ☐

  4 Tyson tells Marvin why he's afraid of dogs. ☐

  5 Tyson changes the TV programme to football. ☐

  6 Marvin and Tyson become friends. ☐

  7 Tyson says that his real name is 'Lionel'. ☐

  8 Tyson feels sick. ☐

3 <u>Underline</u> the correct words in each sentence.

  1 Robert *likes / doesn't like* Marvin's grandad.

  2 *Mum / Grandad* invites Tyson to come in.

  3 Tyson heard about *Smelly Vision* in the *school café / classroom*.

  4 Tyson *feels / doesn't feel* afraid when the shower sings.

  5 The next morning *Tyson / Robert* is at Marvin's house.

  6 *Grandad / Marvin* talked to Tyson's mum.

  7 *Marvin / Tyson* had a toy bear when he was younger.

  8 Grandad makes a suit with *drinks / bath water* in it.

4 Are the sentences true (*T*) or false (*F*)?

1 Marvin and Robert watch a food programme. [T]
2 Robert takes the remote control from Marvin's hand. ☐
3 That night Marvin doesn't sleep well. ☐
4 Mum tells Marvin that Tyson's name is 'Lionel'. ☐
5 'Tyson' was the dog that bit Marvin. ☐
6 Grandad says that dogs are afraid of noise. ☐
7 When Tyson sees the dog coming, he closes his eyes. ☐
8 Tyson doesn't like his new suit. ☐

5 Answer the questions.

1 What programme do Marvin and Robert watch?

2 Where does Tyson sit?

3 What programme does Tyson want to watch?

4 Why does Tyson leave Marvin's house?

5 How did Tyson really get his scar?

6 Why is Tyson's suit special?

Glossary

[1]**mad** (page 5) *adjective*   crazy

[2]**gadget** (page 5) *noun*   an object that does a particular job

[3]**tidy up** (page 5) *verb*   to put things in the right place

[4]**bully** (page 7) *noun*   a person who frightens someone who is smaller or weaker

[5]**trainer** (page 10) *noun*   sports shoe

[6]**promise** (page 10) *verb*   to say that you will certainly do something

[7]**trouble** (page 16) *noun*   problems

[8]**throw** (page 17) *verb*   to make something move through the air by pushing it out of your hand

[9]**dustbin** (page 17) *noun*   a large container for rubbish

[10]**smelly** (page 17) *adjective*   having a bad smell

[11]**shake** (page 18) *verb*   if you are shaking, your body makes quick, short movements because you are nervous or frightened

[12]**drop** (page 24) *verb*   to let something fall

[13]**pick up** (page 24) *verb*   to lift something by using your hands

[14]**You're welcome!** (page 30)   you say this as a polite answer when someone thanks you for doing something

[15]**note** (page 32) *noun*   a short letter

[16]**get dressed** (page 36) *verb*   to put on your clothes

[17]**sniff** (page 38) *verb*   to breathe air in through your nose in order to smell something

[18]**backpack** (page 40) *noun*   a bag that you carry on your back

[19]**Bad luck!** (page 46)   you say this to someone when something bad has happened to them

[20]**worried** (page 56) *adjective*   unhappy because you are thinking about bad things that could happen